THE ARTISANAL KITCHEN

GLUTEN-FREE

HOLIDAY
COOKIES

THE ARTISANAL KITCHEN

GLUTEN=FREE
HOLIDAY
COOKIES

MORE THAN 30 RECIPES
TO SWEETEN THE SEASON

Alice Medrich

with Maya Klein

ARTISAN | NEW YORK

CONTENTS

FESTIVE AND FANCY 43

INTRODUCTION

Nothing evokes the holidays quite like an assortment of homemade cookies. Now just imagine a cookie tray, hostess gift, or take-to-school basket that's perfect for today's omnivores and gluten-free eaters alike. Imagine not having to make apologies, special batches of cookies, separate plates, labels, or explanations about who can eat what.

This curated collection was inspired by our love affair with cookies of all kinds, our passion for new tastes as well as tradition, and our obsession with flavorful non-wheat flours. We've not only enhanced and updated the cookie repertoire with whole-grain flours, we've also taken the uncertainty (and unhappy surprises) out of gluten-free baking with simple, well-tested recipes that all kinds of dessert fans will enjoy. Some cookies are comfy and familiar, some are entirely new inventions, and all are delicious! You'll find sturdy cookies to pack and send, delicate cookies that impress, spiced cookies to warm and satiate, and long-keeping cookies, all with clear instructions, do-ahead tips, and storage information.

You'll love the simplicity of easy new classics like the super-spicy Classic Ginger Cookies, Double Oatmeal Cookies for true oat lovers, and Chocolate Chip Cookies with crispy edges, tender middles, and a hint of butterscotch. There are two kinds of coconut cookies, myriad butter cookies and shortbreads, and brownies that are blond, kid-friendly, or decadently ultra-chocolate.

Go ahead, show off a little with Chocolate-Mint Sandwich Cookies, jam-filled Buckwheat Linzer Cookies, and dainty Oat and Almond Tuiles. Don't miss over-the-top Chunky Double-Chocolate Coconut Meringues, tender Nutty Thumbprint Cookies, and Chestnut Meringue Mushrooms that melt in your mouth. And no holiday season would be complete without cutout cookies to decorate with kids—here you'll even find a lickety-split slice-and-bake version of them with lots of creative flavor options.

Whether you are an occasional baker or a passionate pastry chef, cookies are gloriously easy, festive, and fun. With this holiday collection, we wish you happy baking and *bon appétit*!

TEN TIPS FOR SUCCESS

Working with new methods and new flours that behave in new or unexpected ways means that the little details are more important than ever! Here are the top ten.

1. **Keep flours fresh:** Store whole-grain and other perishable flours (like nut flours) in airtight containers in the fridge or freezer to prevent them from turning rancid. Bring to room temperature before opening the container to avoid condensation.

2. **Do your mise en place like a pro:** Measuring all your ingredients before you start ensures that you have what you need and will not forget an ingredient along the way.

3. **Measure accurately:** A scale is always the best way to measure ingredients, but if you must use measuring cups, follow this method: Set the appropriate-size measuring cup on a piece of wax paper on the counter. If the flour in the canister or the bag is very compacted, loosen it gently with a spoon (don't overdo it, though, or your measure will be too light). Pour or spoon the flour lightly into the cup until it is heaped above the rim. Without tapping or shaking the cup or compacting the flour, sweep the flour level with the rim using a straightedge.

4. **Check your oven temperature:** Put an oven thermometer in the center of the oven and make sure it registers the same temperature that you set. If not, adjust the dial. Better yet, get a professional to calibrate your oven. For convection ovens, consult the manual that came with the oven; you may be instructed to use a lower temperature and check for doneness early.

5. **Position your oven racks:** Things bake differently on different racks. Unless you're using a convection oven, always position the oven racks at the level called for in each recipe and rotate pans if called for as well. For convection ovens, consult the oven manual for rack position advice.

6. Mix it right: Some recipes need vigorous beating or whisking; some need only delicate folding. Use the utensil, type of action, and speed called for. Where it matters, mixing times are given to help you get it right.

7. Rest and hydrate: Some flours in some recipes need time to absorb liquid from the batter so that the finished cookies or bars don't taste raw or feel gritty on the palate. Hydration is built into the recipes where necessary. Some recipes may call for resting the dough for at least 2 hours, or even overnight—and the recipe won't call for it unless the payoff is worth the wait.

8. Use the type and size of pans called for: Metal and glass baking pans bake differently. Round or square, a 9-inch pan may not seem much bigger than an 8-inch one, but it has 25 percent more surface area. If your pan is too large, your bars will be thinner than you expect and overbaked when your timer goes off.

9. Always cool cookies completely before frosting or wrapping (unless instructed otherwise).

10. Create like a pastry chef: The best way to make a new successful recipe from an existing but unfamiliar one is to first follow the original recipe as written, so that you know what the flavors and textures are like when the recipe works. Then change one thing at a time. If you make too many changes at once, you will never know which change was responsible for the failure.

    Bonus Tip: Recipes that call for white rice flour give you the option of using Thai white rice flour (see Resources, page 90). The Thai flour is ultra-fine; you will note that while the weight required for a recipe remains the same, the cup measurement is different because less Thai flour fits into a cup. Each recipe gives both weight and cup measures accordingly.

NEW
CLASSICS

CHOCOLATE CHIP COOKIES

Oat and brown rice flours give these cookies extra butterscotch flavor—and a beautiful butterscotch color as well for a classic and elegant addition to your holiday dessert spread. You will love the buttery, crunchy edges and delicate cakey interiors. Resting the dough overnight—or for at least a couple of hours—makes these cookies especially good. **MAKES ABOUT 5 DOZEN 3½-INCH COOKIES**

1¼ cups (125 grams) gluten-free oat flour

1 cup (135 grams) brown rice flour

¼ cup plus 2 tablespoons (65 grams) potato starch

½ teaspoon salt

½ teaspoon baking soda

¾ teaspoon xanthan gum

½ pound (2 sticks/225 grams) unsalted butter, melted

¾ cup (150 grams) granulated sugar

¾ cup (150 grams) packed dark brown sugar

1 teaspoon pure vanilla extract

2 large eggs

2 cups (340 grams) chocolate chips or chunks or hand-chopped chocolate

1 cup (100 grams) walnuts or pecans, coarsely chopped

EQUIPMENT

Baking sheets, lined with foil (dull side up) or greased

Combine the flours, potato starch, salt, baking soda, and xanthan gum in a medium bowl and mix thoroughly with a whisk.

In a large bowl, mix the melted butter, sugars, and vanilla. Whisk in the eggs. Stir in the flour mixture. With a rubber spatula, mix the batter briskly for about 45 seconds (to activate the binding power of the xanthan gum—the more you mix, the chewier and less crunchy the cookies will be). Stir in the chocolate chips and nuts. If possible, let the dough stand for 1 to 2 hours, or (better still) cover and refrigerate it overnight.

Position racks in the upper and lower thirds of the oven and preheat the oven to 375°F.

Scoop 2 tablespoons of dough per cookie and place 2 inches apart on the prepared baking sheets. Bake until the cookies are golden brown, 12 to 14 minutes. Rotate the pans from top to bottom and from front to back halfway through the baking time. For lined pans, set the pans or just the liners on racks to cool; for greased pans, use a metal spatula to transfer the cookies to racks. Cool the cookies completely before stacking or storing. They will keep in an airtight container for several days.

Pecan Spice Cookies

Add 2 teaspoons ground cinnamon, ½ teaspoon ground nutmeg, ½ teaspoon ground cloves, and ½ teaspoon ground ginger with the sugar. Omit the chocolate chips and use 2 cups (200 grams) lightly toasted pecan pieces for the nuts.

Nibby Nut and Raisin Cookies

Omit the chocolate chips. Add 1 cup (140 grams) raisins and ⅔ cup (75 grams) roasted cacao nibs with the walnuts.

CLASSIC GINGER COOKIES

The flavor of oat flour is so perfect with the ginger and other warm spices, you will never look back. These easy one-bowl ginger cookies are the perfect choice for a last-minute gathering and may become one of your favorites! **MAKES ABOUT 50 COOKIES**

½ cup (100 grams) granulated sugar

⅓ cup (65 grams) packed brown sugar

2½ teaspoons ground ginger

1½ teaspoons ground cinnamon

½ teaspoon ground allspice

2 teaspoons baking soda

¼ teaspoon salt

¼ cup (85 grams) unsulfured mild or full-flavored molasses (not blackstrap)

8 tablespoons (1 stick/ 115 grams) unsalted butter, melted and kept lukewarm

2 large egg whites

2¾ cups (275 grams) gluten-free oat flour

¾ cup (115 grams/4 ounces) ginger chips or crystallized ginger, cut into ¼-inch dice, shaken in a coarse strainer to remove loose sugar

About ½ cup (100 grams) granulated or coarse sugar, such as turbinado, for rolling

If you are baking the cookies right away, position racks in the upper and lower thirds of the oven and preheat the oven to 350°F.

In a medium bowl, mix the ½ cup granulated sugar, the brown sugar, ground ginger, cinnamon, allspice, baking soda, salt, molasses, butter, and egg whites until blended. Stir in the flour.

When the flour is no longer visible, beat the dough briskly with a spatula or a wooden spoon, about 40 strokes, to aerate it slightly. Stir in the ginger chips. The dough will be very soft. If possible, chill it for an hour or two to firm it up, or (better still) cover and refrigerate it overnight for the best flavor and texture.

Form the dough into 1-inch balls (15 grams each). Roll the balls in granulated or coarse sugar and place them 2 inches apart on the baking sheets. Bake for 10 to 12 minutes, or until the cookies puff up and crack on the surface and then begin to deflate in the oven. Rotate the pans from top to bottom and from front to back halfway through the baking time. For chewier cookies, remove them from the oven when at least half or more of the cookies have begun to deflate; for crunchier edges with chewy centers, bake for a minute or so longer.

EQUIPMENT

Baking sheets, lined with
parchment paper or unlined
and ungreased

For lined pans, set the pans or just the liners on
racks to cool; for unlined pans, use a metal spatula
to transfer the cookies to racks. Cool the cookies
completely before storing. They will keep in an
airtight container for several days.

VARIATION: Molasses Spice Cookies

Substitute ¾ cup plus 2 tablespoons (175 grams)
light or dark brown sugar for the granulated and brown
sugar in the dough. Substitute ½ teaspoon ground
cloves for the allspice. Substitute 1 large egg for the
egg whites. Omit the ginger chips. Makes about
40 cookies.

NUTTY THUMBPRINT COOKIES

These thumbprint cookies are actually a filled version of ultra-tender, not-too-sweet Russian tea cakes (also known as Mexican wedding cakes), which are similar to the divine crescent-shaped Austrian cookies called *Vanillekipferl*. See the variations for instructions on how to make both. **MAKES THIRTY-SIX TO FORTY 1½-INCH COOKIES**

1½ cups (150 grams) walnuts or pecans

¼ cup plus 2 tablespoons (55 grams) white rice flour
—OR—
½ cup plus 1 tablespoon (55 grams) Thai white rice flour

1¼ cups plus 2 tablespoons (140 grams) gluten-free oat flour

¼ teaspoon salt

⅛ teaspoon baking soda

⅓ cup (65 grams) granulated sugar

¼ cup (60 grams) cream cheese, cold, cut into chunks

12 tablespoons (1½ sticks/ 170 grams) unsalted butter, slightly softened and cut into chunks

1 teaspoon pure vanilla extract

¼ cup (20 grams) powdered sugar for dusting

¼ cup chocolate frosting, Nutella, jam, preserves, lemon curd, or dulce de leche or cajeta (see Note)

continued

Put the nuts, rice and oat flours, salt, baking soda, and granulated sugar in the food processor. Pulse until the nuts are coarsely chopped. Add the cream cheese, butter, and vanilla. Process just until the dough forms a ball around the blade.

Wrap the dough and refrigerate it for at least 2 hours, but preferably overnight.

Position racks in the upper and lower thirds of the oven and preheat the oven to 325°F.

Shape slightly rounded tablespoons of dough into 1-inch balls. Place the cookies at least 1½ inches apart on the prepared baking sheets. Bake for 15 to 20 minutes, until golden brown on the bottom. Rotate the pans from top to bottom and from front to back halfway through the baking time. As soon as the cookies are out of the oven, press the handle of a wooden spoon about halfway into the center of each one.

Set the pans or just the liners on racks to finish cooling. Let the cookies cool completely before storing. Unfilled cookies will keep in an airtight container for at least 2 weeks. Use the strainer to dust the cookies with powdered sugar. Cookies may be filled in advance with frosting or Nutella, but moister fillings should be added shortly before serving to avoid making cookies soggy.

continued

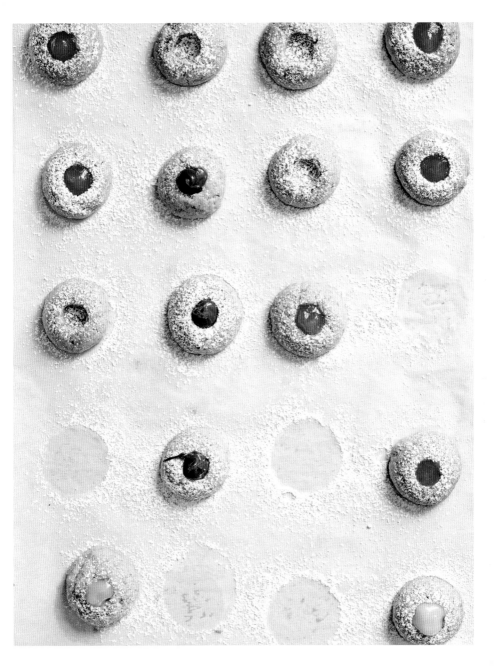

Food processor fitted with the steel blade

Baking sheets, lined with parchment paper

Fine-mesh strainer

NOTE: *Cajeta, or goat's-milk caramel, is available in cans or squeeze bottles from better supermarkets and Hispanic groceries.*

VARIATIONS

Russian Tea Cakes/Mexican Wedding Cakes

Simply skip the "poking" and filling steps and dust the cookies with powdered sugar.

Vanillekipferl

Substitute 1½ cups (215 grams) blanched or natural almonds, or use 2 cups (200 grams) purchased almond meal or flour. Increase the vanilla to 1½ teaspoons. If using nut meal (or nut flour), pulse it with the dry ingredients just to mix (rather than pulverize) before adding the rest of the ingredients. Shape the dough into fat crescents and skip the poking step.

Nutty Sablés and Sandwiches

Any nut variation of this recipe makes divine sablés and sandwich cookies, filled with dulce de leche or cajeta. You can substitute an equal volume of almonds or hazelnuts for the walnuts or pecans, if desired. Make the dough as directed, but process the nuts until finely ground rather than coarsely chopped. Form the dough into a 10- to 12-inch log 2 inches in diameter. Wrap well and chill for at least 2 hours, or overnight. Slice into scant ¼-inch-thick slices and place them 1½ inches apart on the prepared baking sheets. Bake for 8 to 10 minutes, until golden brown at the edges and deep brown underneath. Cool as directed. Serve sablés plain, or sandwich 2 cookies with a generous dab of dulce de leche or cajeta. The filled cookies will soften as they stand, but they are good crunchy or soft. They will keep in an airtight container for at least a week.

DOUBLE OATMEAL COOKIES

These oatmeal cookies—made with oats *and* oat flour—are truly for oat lovers! You can adjust the chewiness of your cookies by mixing the batter more or mixing it less. Baking them on foil (instead of parchment) or directly on a greased pan produces some lovely crunchy edges on these otherwise chewy cookies.

MAKES ABOUT THIRTY-TWO 3½-INCH COOKIES

1¼ cups (125 grams) gluten-free oat flour

2 cups (190 grams) gluten-free rolled oats

½ teaspoon salt

1 teaspoon baking soda

¾ teaspoon xanthan gum

½ pound (2 sticks/225 grams) unsalted butter, melted

¾ cup (150 grams) granulated sugar

¾ cup (150 grams) packed light brown sugar

1 teaspoon ground cinnamon

¼ teaspoon freshly grated nutmeg

1 teaspoon pure vanilla extract

2 large eggs

Generous 1 cup (115 grams) coarsely chopped walnuts

1 cup (140 grams) raisins

EQUIPMENT

Baking sheets, lined with foil (dull side up) or greased

Combine the oat flour, rolled oats, salt, baking soda, and xanthan gum in a medium bowl and whisk until blended.

In a large bowl, mix the butter, sugars, cinnamon, nutmeg, and vanilla. Whisk in the eggs. Stir in the oat mixture and mix the batter briskly with a spatula for about 1 minute (to activate the binding power of the xanthan gum—the more you mix, the chewier and less crunchy the cookies will be). Stir in the nuts and raisins. Let the dough stand for at least 1 hour, but preferably 2 hours; or (better still) cover and refrigerate it overnight for the best flavor and texture.

Position racks in the upper and lower thirds of the oven and preheat the oven to 325°F.

Scoop 2 tablespoons of dough per cookie and place 2 inches apart on the prepared baking sheets. Bake for 16 to 20 minutes, until the cookies are deep golden brown. Rotate the pans from top to bottom and from front to back halfway through the baking time. For lined pans, set the pans or just the liners on racks to cool; for greased pans, use a metal spatula to transfer the cookies to racks. Cool the cookies completely before stacking or storing. They will keep in an airtight container for several days.

BROWN SUGAR PECAN COOKIES

These plain, dense, seemingly rustic cookies will sneak up on you. They are adapted from a recipe in Rosetta Costantino's compelling book *Southern Italian Desserts*. Authentic *dolci di noci*, made with walnuts and white sugar and without salt, are quintessentially Italian, and very, very good. Here, they have an American flavor twist with pecans instead of walnuts, a bit of brown sugar, and some salt.

MAKES THIRTY-TWO 1½-INCH COOKIES

2¾ cups (285 grams) pecan halves or large pieces

½ cup (100 grams) granulated sugar

½ cup (100 grams) packed light or dark brown sugar

¼ teaspoon salt

1 large egg

EQUIPMENT

Food processor fitted with the steel blade

Baking sheet, lined with parchment paper

Position a rack in the center of the oven and preheat the oven to 350°F.

Put the nuts, both sugars, and salt in the food processor. Process until the nuts are finely ground. Add the egg and process to a coarse, sticky dough.

Remove the dough and knead it with your hands a few times to be sure it is evenly mixed. Pat the dough into a 6-by-4-inch rectangle about 1 inch thick. Use a straightedge to square the sides. Cut the rectangle lengthwise into 4 strips and crosswise into 8 to make 32 equal pieces. Roll each piece into a ball or a log shape and space the pieces 1 inch apart on the prepared baking sheet.

Bake for 12 to 15 minutes, or until the surface of the cookies is partially browned and the bottoms are deep brown. Set the baking sheet on a rack to cool. The cooled cookies will keep in an airtight container for 2 weeks.

VARIATION: Nutty Peanut Cookies

Substitute 2¼ cups (255 grams) roasted unsalted peanuts for the pecans. Increase the salt to ⅜ teaspoon and add 1 teaspoon pure vanilla extract with the egg.

CRUNCHY COCONUT COOKIES

Crisp *and* chewy! Serve these wafers with a dish of pineapple or mango sherbet or silky rice pudding. **MAKES 3 DOZEN 2-INCH COOKIES**

Scant ½ cup (50 grams) coconut flour

1¾ cups (150 grams) unsweetened dried shredded coconut

¼ teaspoon baking powder

½ teaspoon salt

6 tablespoons (85 grams) unsalted butter, very soft

1 cup plus 2 tablespoons (225 grams) sugar

1 teaspoon pure vanilla extract

1 large egg white

¼ cup water

EQUIPMENT

Baking sheets, lined with parchment paper

Combine the coconut flour, coconut, baking powder, salt, butter, sugar, vanilla, egg white, and water in a large bowl and mix until all the ingredients are well incorporated. Form the mixture into a 10-inch log 2 inches in diameter on a sheet of wax or parchment paper. Wrap the log in the paper, keeping it as cylindrical as possible. Chill for at least 2 hours and up to 3 days, or wrap airtight and freeze for up to 3 months. Thaw before using.

Position racks in the upper and lower thirds of the oven and preheat the oven to 350°F.

Use a thin serrated knife to cut the dough into slices a little less than ¼ inch thick. Place the slices 1 inch apart on the prepared baking sheets.

Bake for 12 to 14 minutes, until the cookies are golden on the bottom and browned at the edges; rotate the pans from top to bottom and from front to back halfway through the baking time. Place the pans on racks, or slide the liners from the pans onto racks to cool completely. The cookies will keep in an airtight container for up to 1 week.

VARIATION: Crunchy Coconut Cookies with Bittersweet Chocolate

Add 2 ounces (55 grams) finely chopped semisweet or bittersweet chocolate along with the coconut.

CRISPY COCONUT WAFERS

There are only five ingredients and not a bit of flour in these easy-peasy, super-crunchy cookies. Keep them on hand to dunk, smear with peanut butter, use to make ice cream sammies, or dip in dark chocolate. **MAKES ABOUT 3 DOZEN 3½-INCH COOKIES**

3 tablespoons (45 grams) unsalted butter, melted, plus more for greasing the foil

3 large egg whites

1 cup plus 2 tablespoons (100 grams) unsweetened dried shredded coconut

½ cup (100 grams) sugar

¼ teaspoon salt

EQUIPMENT

Baking sheets

Line the baking sheets with regular foil (dull side up) and grease the foil lightly but thoroughly with butter. Or line the baking sheets with nonstick foil (nonstick side up; see Note).

In a medium bowl, mix the egg whites with the coconut, sugar, and salt until well blended. Stir in the melted butter. Let the batter rest for at least 15 minutes to allow the coconut to absorb moisture (or cover and store it in the refrigerator for up to 3 days).

Position racks in the upper and lower thirds of the oven and preheat the oven to 300°F.

Stir the batter well. Drop level tablespoons 3 inches apart on the prepared baking sheets. Spread the batter to a diameter of 3½ inches (about ¼ inch thick).

Bake for 20 to 25 minutes, or until the cookies are mostly golden brown on top—a few pale patches are okay. Rotate the pans from top to bottom and from front to back about halfway through the baking time. If the cookies are not baked enough, they will not be completely crisp when cool.

Slide the foil sheets onto racks and let the cookies cool slightly or even completely before removing them.

continued

To retain crispness, put the cookies in an airtight container as soon as they are cool. They will keep for at least 1 month.

NOTES: *Nonstick foil is the easier type to use and can be wiped and reused over and over again.*

You can sprinkle the cookies before baking with a pinch of black or white sesame seeds, or substitute ½ cup (55 grams) finely chopped pecans or almonds (with ½ teaspoon pure almond extract) for an equal amount of the coconut.

SORGHUM CINNAMON STICKS

Imagine superlight stick-shaped biscotti dredged in spicy sugar. These are addictive and noisy to eat. If you like Indian spices or just want to add a touch of complexity to the flavors here, add a pinch of garam masala to the cinnamon sugar. Or for some seasonal flair, try pumpkin pie spice. **MAKES 2 DOZEN STICKS**

3 tablespoons (45 grams) unsalted butter

¾ cup plus 1 tablespoon (110 grams) sorghum flour

¼ cup plus 2 tablespoons (75 grams) sugar

Generous ⅛ teaspoon salt

½ teaspoon baking powder

2 large eggs, at room temperature

Cinnamon sugar: 2 tablespoons sugar mixed with ½ teaspoon cinnamon (optional: a pinch of garam masala or pumpkin pie spice)

EQUIPMENT

Skillet at least 12 inches wide

Baking sheet, lined with parchment paper or foil

Stand mixer with whisk attachment, or handheld mixer

8-inch square pan, bottom lined with parchment paper

Melt the butter in a large heavy-bottomed skillet. Take the pan off the heat, add the sorghum flour, and stir to coat all the flour grains with butter. The mixture will have the consistency of slightly damp sand. Return the skillet to the stove and cook over medium-high heat, stirring constantly with a heatproof spatula or fork; scrape the bottom and sides of the pan, turning the flour, and spread or rake to redistribute it continuously so that it toasts evenly. Continue to cook and stir until the mixture colors slightly and smells toasted; it may begin to smoke a little. Toasting the flour will take 4 to 6 minutes. Scrape the flour onto the prepared baking sheet and spread it out to cool while preheating the oven.

Position a rack in the lower third of the oven and preheat the oven to 350°F.

Combine the sugar, salt, baking powder, and eggs in the bowl of the stand mixer fitted with the whisk attachment (or in a large mixing bowl if using a handheld mixer). Beat on high speed for 3 to 5 minutes, until thick and light. Poke and mash any large lumps in the toasted flour and then lift the liner with both hands to pour the toasted flour over the egg mixture. Keep the unlined baking sheet handy for later. Fold just until evenly mixed. Scrape the batter into the prepared baking pan and spread it evenly; it will be a thin layer only about ½ inch deep.

Bake for 20 to 25 minutes, or until golden brown and springy to the touch. Set the pan on a rack to cool. Leave the oven on, but reduce the temperature to 300°F.

Slide a slim knife around the edges of the pan to detach it. Invert the pan onto a rack and peel off the liner. Place the baked sheet right side up on a cutting board. Cut it in half with a sharp serrated knife. Cut each half crosswise into slices a scant ¾ inch wide.

Put the cinnamon sugar in a shallow dish and gently dredge the sticks liberally on all sides. Arrange the slices slightly apart on the unlined baking sheet. Bake for 20 to 25 minutes, or until slightly golden brown. Rotate the pan from top to bottom and from front to back about halfway through the baking time. Cool the cookies completely before storing. They will keep in an airtight container for several weeks.

NOTE: *If you want to double the recipe, use a 9-by-13-inch baking pan. Toasting the sorghum flour may take 10 to 12 minutes and require a skillet at least 14 inches wide (wider is better). The larger amount of flour may clump while toasting; if necessary, mash out lumps with a fork while the flour is cooling. It may be easier to toast the flour in two batches instead, then proceed as directed.*

NUTMEG SHORTBREAD

If nutmeg is one of your favorite flavors, these cookies are for you! They definitely belong on a holiday treat tray, and do serve them with eggnog. **MAKES 40 COOKIES**

---

1 cup plus 2 tablespoons (150 grams) sorghum flour

⅓ cup plus 1 tablespoon (60 grams) white rice flour —OR— ½ cup plus 1 tablespoon (60 grams) Thai white rice flour

½ cup (100 grams) sugar

¾ teaspoon freshly grated nutmeg

Rounded ¼ teaspoon salt

12 tablespoons (1½ sticks/ 170 grams) unsalted butter, slightly softened and cut into chunks

¼ cup (60 grams) cream cheese

1 tablespoon water

1 teaspoon pure vanilla extract

Nutmeg sugar: 1 tablespoon sugar mixed with ½ teaspoon grated nutmeg

EQUIPMENT

Food processor fitted with the steel blade (optional)

Baking sheets, lined with parchment paper

To make the dough by hand, put the sorghum and rice flours, ½ cup sugar, nutmeg, and salt in a large bowl and whisk until thoroughly blended. Add the butter chunks, cream cheese, water, and vanilla. Use a fork or the back of a large spoon to mash and mix the ingredients together until all are blended into a smooth, soft dough.

To make the dough in a food processor, put the sorghum and rice flours, ½ cup sugar, nutmeg, and salt in the food processor and pulse to mix. Add the butter chunks, cream cheese, water, and vanilla. Pulse until the mixture forms a smooth, soft dough. Scrape the bowl and mix in any stray flour at the bottom of the bowl with your fingers.

On a sheet of wax or parchment paper set on a baking sheet, press the dough into an even 8-by-10-inch rectangle about ½ inch thick. Cover the dough with plastic wrap and refrigerate it for at least 2 hours and up to 3 days (see Note).

Position racks in the upper and lower thirds of the oven and preheat the oven to 325°F.

Sprinkle the dough with the nutmeg sugar. Cut the dough lengthwise into 1-inch strips, then crosswise into 2-inch lengths and place them an inch apart on the prepared baking sheets. Bake for 20 to 25 minutes, until the cookies are golden brown at the edges. Rotate the pans from top to bottom and from front to back a little over halfway through the baking time. Place the pans on racks, or slide the liners from the pans onto racks to cool. Cool the cookies completely before stacking or storing. They will keep in an airtight container for at least 2 weeks.

NOTE: *Do-ahead for best flavor and texture: Let the dough rest and hydrate overnight in the fridge before baking, and store cookies for at least 1 day before serving.*

SALTED PEANUT SHORTIES

These tender melt-in-your-mouth shortbread cookies are loaded with salted peanuts and scented with bourbon. For a special treat, sandwich them just before serving with dulce de leche, melted chocolate (see page 62), or strawberry jam.
MAKES 45 TO 50 COOKIES

---

2 cups (225 grams) roasted or dry-roasted salted peanuts

1 cup plus 2 tablespoons (150 grams) sorghum flour

⅓ cup plus 1 tablespoon (60 grams) white rice flour
—OR—
½ cup plus 1 tablespoon (60 grams) Thai white rice flour

⅔ cup (135 grams) sugar

12 tablespoons (1½ sticks/ 170 grams) unsalted butter, slightly softened and cut into chunks

¼ cup (60 grams) cream cheese

2 tablespoons bourbon or 1 tablespoon water

1 teaspoon pure vanilla extract

EQUIPMENT

Food processor fitted with the steel blade

Baking sheets, lined with parchment paper

Put the peanuts, sorghum and rice flours, and sugar in the food processor. Pulse until the peanuts are mostly pulverized, but not too finely. Add the butter chunks, cream cheese, bourbon or water, and vanilla. Pulse until the mixture forms a smooth, soft dough. Scrape the bowl and blend in any stray flour at the bottom of the bowl with your fingers. On a sheet of wax or parchment paper, shape the dough into a 12-inch log about 2 inches in diameter. Wrap the dough and refrigerate it for at least 2 hours, but preferably overnight (see Note).

Position racks in the upper and lower thirds of the oven and preheat the oven to 325°F.

Slice the chilled cookie dough into ¼-inch slices and place them 1 inch apart on the prepared baking sheets. Bake for 20 to 25 minutes, until the cookies are golden brown at the edges. Rotate the pans from top to bottom and from front to back a little over halfway through the baking time. Place the pans on racks, or slide the liners from the pans onto racks to cool. Cool the cookies completely before stacking or storing. They will keep in an airtight container for at least 2 weeks.

Coffee Walnut Shorties

Substitute 1 generous cup (115 grams) walnuts,
1 teaspoon finely ground coffee beans (regular, not
espresso roast), and ½ teaspoon salt for the peanuts.
Use water instead of bourbon.

Nibby Walnut Shorties

Substitute 1 generous cup (115 grams) walnuts and
½ teaspoon salt for the peanuts. Process only
until the nuts are chopped medium-fine instead of
pulverized. Add ¼ cup roasted cacao nibs with the
remaining ingredients. Use water instead of bourbon.

NOTE: *Do-ahead for best flavor and texture: Let the dough rest
and hydrate overnight in the fridge before baking, and store
cookies for at least 1 day before serving.*

BUCKWHEAT SHORTBREAD COOKIES

These melt-in-your-mouth cookies have a perfect tender sandy texture. Serve them with a bowl of fresh blackberries (or other cane berries) and cream. Or turn them into sandwich or linzer cookies (see page 76) filled with a little blackberry or plum preserves or prune butter. **MAKES ABOUT 3 DOZEN 2-INCH COOKIES**

¼ cup plus 2 tablespoons (55 grams) white rice flour
—OR—
½ cup plus 1 tablespoon (55 grams) Thai white rice flour

½ cup plus 2 tablespoons (70 grams) buckwheat flour

⅔ cup (65 grams) gluten-free oat flour

¼ teaspoon salt

⅛ teaspoon baking soda

½ cup (100 grams) sugar

¼ cup (60 grams) cream cheese, cut into chunks

12 tablespoons (1½ sticks/ 170 grams) unsalted butter, cut into chunks and softened

1 tablespoon water

EQUIPMENT

Food processor fitted with the steel blade (optional)

Baking sheets, lined with parchment paper

To make the dough by hand, put the rice, buckwheat, and oat flours, salt, baking soda, and sugar in a large bowl and whisk until thoroughly blended. Add the cream cheese, butter, and water. Use a fork or the back of a large spoon to mash and mix the ingredients together until all are blended into a smooth, soft dough.

To make the dough in a food processor, put the rice, buckwheat, and oat flours, salt, baking soda, and sugar in the food processor. Pulse to mix thoroughly. Add the cream cheese, butter, and water. Process just until the mixture forms a ball of smooth, soft dough. Scrape the bowl and blend in any stray flour at the bottom with your fingers.

Scrape the dough onto a sheet of wax or parchment paper and form it into a 10-inch log about 1¾ inches in diameter. Wrap tightly in the wax paper and refrigerate for at least 2 hours, but preferably longer or overnight.

Position racks in the upper and lower thirds of the oven and preheat the oven to 325°F.

Use a sharp knife to cut the cold logs of dough into ¼-inch slices. Place the cookies at least 1½ inches apart on the prepared baking sheets. Bake for 20 to 25 minutes, rotating the pans from top to bottom and from front to back about halfway through the baking time, until the cookies are slightly darker brown at the edges and well browned on the bottom.

Set the pans or just the liners on racks to cool. Cool the cookies completely before stacking or storing. They will keep in an airtight container for at least 2 weeks.

CHESTNUT AND PINE NUT SHORTBREAD

These delicate and not-too-sweet little shortbread cookies are covered in toasted pine nuts—a resonant flavor with chestnuts. They taste just like Italy to us! Serve them with a little vin santo if you are in Italian mode, or give them as a gift to a sophisticated pal. For a sensational variation, add a cup (100 grams) of chopped walnuts to the dough. **MAKES 45 TO 50 COOKIES**

1½ cups (150 grams) chestnut flour

⅓ cup plus 1 tablespoon (60 grams) white rice flour —OR— ½ cup plus 1 tablespoon (60 grams) Thai white rice flour

½ cup (100 grams) sugar

Rounded ¼ teaspoon salt

12 tablespoons (1½ sticks/ 170 grams) unsalted butter, slightly softened and cut into chunks

¼ cup (60 grams) cream cheese

⅓ cup (40 grams) pine nuts

EQUIPMENT

Food processor fitted with the steel blade (optional)

Baking sheets, lined with parchment paper

To make the dough by hand, put the chestnut and rice flours, sugar, and salt in a large bowl and whisk until thoroughly blended. Add the butter chunks and cream cheese. Use a fork or the back of a large spoon to mash and mix the ingredients together until all are blended into a smooth, soft dough.

To make the dough in a food processor, put the chestnut and rice flours, sugar, and salt in the food processor and pulse to mix. Add the butter chunks and cream cheese. Pulse until the mixture forms a smooth, soft dough. Scrape the bowl and mix in any stray flour at the bottom of the bowl with your fingers.

Press the dough into an even 9-inch square about ½ inch thick on a sheet of wax or parchment paper set on a baking sheet or smaller flat surface. Sprinkle the pine nuts evenly over the dough, then press them gently to embed them in the dough. Cover the dough and refrigerate it for at least 2 hours or, wrapped in plastic, up to 3 days.

Position racks in the upper and lower thirds of the oven and preheat the oven to 325°F.

Cut the dough into 1¼-inch squares and place them 1 inch apart on the prepared baking sheets. Bake for 20 to 25 minutes, until the cookies are golden brown at the edges. Rotate the pans from top to bottom and from front to back a little over halfway through the baking time. Place the pans on racks, or slide the liners from the pans onto racks to cool. Cool the cookies completely before stacking or storing. They will keep in an airtight container for at least 2 weeks.

NOTE: *For round cookies, cut the dough with a cookie cutter, then push the scraps back together and cut again; don't worry about cookies becoming tough from reworking the scraps. Or form the dough into a log, wrap, chill, and slice.*

NEW CLASSIC BLONDIES

Oat flour brings its own natural butterscotch flavor to this childhood treat. These classic bars will be as welcome on a holiday party dessert table as they are as an after-school snack. MAKES SIXTEEN 2-INCH BLONDIES

⅔ cup (60 grams) gluten-free oat flour

⅓ cup plus 1 tablespoon (60 grams) white rice flour
—OR—
½ cup plus 1 tablespoon (60 grams) Thai white rice flour

3 tablespoons (30 grams) potato starch

¼ teaspoon baking soda

¼ teaspoon xanthan gum

Rounded ¼ teaspoon salt

8 tablespoons (1 stick/ 115 grams) unsalted butter, melted and kept warm

⅓ cup (65 grams) packed light brown sugar

⅓ cup (65 grams) granulated sugar

1 large egg

¾ teaspoon pure vanilla extract

¾ cup (75 grams) walnut pieces

¾ cup (130 grams) semisweet or bittersweet chocolate chips

EQUIPMENT

8-inch square pan, bottom and all four sides lined with parchment paper or foil

Position a rack in the lower third of the oven and preheat the oven to 350°F.

In a small bowl, whisk the oat and rice flours, potato starch, baking soda, xanthan gum, and salt until thoroughly blended. Set aside.

Mix the butter and brown and granulated sugars in a medium bowl. Use a spatula or a wooden spoon to beat in the egg and vanilla. Stir in the flour mixture just until moistened, then beat about 20 strokes to aerate the batter slightly. Stir in half of the walnuts and half of the chocolate chips. Spread the batter in the prepared pan. Scatter the remaining walnuts and chocolate chips evenly over the top.

Bake for 20 to 25 minutes, or until the nuts look toasted, the top is golden brown, and the edges have pulled away from the sides of the pan. Cool in the pan on a rack. Lift the ends of the parchment or foil and transfer to a cutting board. Use a long sharp knife to cut into 16 squares. The blondies will keep in an airtight container for 3 to 4 days.

ALMOND AND BROWN RICE BROWNIES

Much more kid friendly than Bittersweet Teff Brownies (page 40), these brownies are far less intense but still dark, gooey, and super chocolaty.

MAKES SIXTEEN 2-INCH BROWNIES

½ cup (70 grams) whole almonds, or ¾ cup (70 grams) almond flour/meal

¼ cup plus 2 tablespoons (50 grams) brown rice flour

6 ounces (170 grams) 60% to 62% cacao dark chocolate, coarsely chopped

6 tablespoons (85 grams) unsalted butter, cut into chunks

½ teaspoon salt

⅔ cup (130 grams) sugar

1 teaspoon pure vanilla extract

2 large eggs, cold

1 cup (100 grams) walnut or pecan pieces (optional)

EQUIPMENT

Food processor fitted with the steel blade (optional)

8-inch square metal baking pan, bottom and all four sides lined with foil

Position a rack in the lower third of the oven and preheat the oven to 325°F.

If using whole almonds, put them in the food processor with the rice flour and pulse until the nuts are finely ground. If using almond flour, simply mix it in a small bowl with the rice flour. Set aside.

Melt the chocolate with the butter in a medium stainless steel bowl set directly in a wide skillet of barely simmering water. Stir frequently until the mixture is melted and hot to the touch.

Remove the bowl and stir in the salt, sugar, and vanilla. Let cool until the mixture is lukewarm. Stir in the eggs one at a time. Add the almond-flour mixture and stir until moistened, then mix briskly for about 40 strokes. Stir in the walnuts or pecans, if using.

Scrape the batter into the prepared pan and spread it evenly. Bake for 20 to 25 minutes, or until the brownies are slightly puffed all over and a toothpick inserted in the center comes out moist but clean.

Cool in the pan on a rack. Lift the foil edges to transfer the brownies to a cutting board. Cut into 16 squares. The brownies will keep in an airtight container at room temperature for 2 to 3 days.

BITTERSWEET TEFF BROWNIES

These moist and deeply chocolate brownies have a light, rather elegant melt-in-your-mouth texture. If you need something dressier than brownies, bake the batter in a 9-inch round pan and serve wedges with whipped cream—and perhaps a scattering of seasonal berries—and call it dessert. MAKES SIXTEEN 2-INCH BROWNIES

10 tablespoons (1¼ sticks/ 140 grams) unsalted butter, cut into chunks

6 ounces (170 grams) 70% cacao dark chocolate, coarsely chopped

1 scant cup (185 grams) sugar

¾ cup (100 grams) teff flour

¼ teaspoon salt

1 teaspoon pure vanilla extract (optional)

3 large eggs, cold

1 cup (100 grams) walnut or pecan pieces (optional)

EQUIPMENT

Handheld mixer

8-inch square pan, bottom and all four sides lined with foil

Position a rack in the lower third of the oven and preheat the oven to 350°F.

Melt the butter with the chocolate in a medium heatproof bowl set directly in a wide skillet of barely simmering water. Stir frequently until the mixture is melted and smooth.

Remove the bowl from the water and cool the mixture to lukewarm. Stir in the sugar, teff flour, salt, and vanilla, if using. Add all the eggs and beat on high speed with the handheld mixer for about 2 minutes. The batter will get thicker and a little lighter in color, like chocolate frosting. Stir in the nuts, if using.

Scrape the batter into the prepared pan and spread it evenly. Bake for 30 to 35 minutes, until a toothpick inserted in the center comes out fairly dry and clean (don't worry; the brownies will be moist even if the toothpick is not).

Cool on a rack. Lift the foil ends to transfer the brownies to a cutting board. Cut into 16 squares. The brownies will keep in an airtight container for 2 to 3 days.

VARIATION: Cocoa Teff Brownies

Cocoa brownies have a softer texture than chocolate brownies. Substitute ¾ cup (65 grams) unsweetened cocoa powder for the chocolate. Increase the butter to 13 tablespoons (185 grams), and increase the sugar to 1 cup plus 3 tablespoons (235 grams).

FESTIVE AND FANCY

BUCKWHEAT WALNUT OR HAZELNUT TUILES

These crispy cookies make a sophisticated addition to a cookie assortment or an elegant counterpoint to a dish of creamy pudding or vanilla ice cream. The earthy, nutty flavor of buckwheat shines here, perfectly partnered with walnuts or hazelnuts—and butter, of course. If you want curved or shaped tuiles, see the box.

Note: Small measures of flour vary too much in weight for delicate cookies. A scale is best. If you do not have a scale, firmly packed and leveled measures will get as close as possible to the correct weights for this particular recipe.

MAKES ABOUT FORTY 3-INCH COOKIES

---

2 tablespoons (28 grams) unsalted butter, melted, plus more for greasing the mats

2 large egg whites

2 teaspoons water

½ cup (100 grams) sugar

2 firmly packed tablespoons (22 grams) white rice flour
—OR—
2 firmly packed tablespoons plus 2 firmly packed teaspoons (22 grams) Thai white rice flour

2 firmly packed tablespoons (22 grams) buckwheat flour

Scant ½ teaspoon salt

⅓ cup (35 grams) finely chopped walnuts or toasted skinned hazelnuts

EQUIPMENT

Baking sheets

Silicone baking mats or nonstick foil

Line the baking sheets with silicone mats or nonstick foil (nonstick side up). For mats, grease them with a very thin (but thorough) coat of melted butter. For nonstick foil, simply smooth the foil to eliminate creases.

In a medium bowl, mix the egg whites with the water, sugar, rice and buckwheat flours, and salt until well blended. Stir in the butter and walnuts. Cover the bowl and let the batter rest for several hours or overnight in the refrigerator to let the flour absorb moisture.

Position racks in the upper and lower thirds of the oven (or one rack in the center if you are baking only one sheet at a time) and preheat the oven to 325°F.

Stir the batter well. Drop level teaspoons 2 inches apart on the prepared baking sheets. Use the back of the spoon to smear the batter into 2½-inch rounds.

Bake, watching carefully, for 12 to 15 minutes, rotating the pans from top to bottom and from front to back

Rolling pin or small cups for shaping (optional; see the box)

about halfway through the baking time, until the tuiles are mostly deep golden brown. If the cookies are not baked enough, they will not be completely crisp when cool.

For flat cookies, you can simply slide the mats or foil sheets onto racks and let the cookies cool on them. Or, if you need to reuse the mats, wait for a minute or two, then transfer the hot cookies to a rack to cool.

To retain crispness, put the cookies in an airtight container as soon as they are cool. They will keep for at least 1 month.

SHAPING TUILES

To make traditional curved tuiles, you must shape the cookies while they are still hot, so you might want to bake only one sheet at a time until you get the hang of it (baking time for a single sheet may be 2 to 3 minutes shorter). Slide a small metal spatula under each cookie immediately, or as soon as you can do so without deforming it. Drape cookies over a rolling pin (anchored so it will not roll) or into custard cups or any small container that will give them an interesting shape. Move the cookies to a cooling rack when they are cool enough to keep their shape. Repeat until all the tuiles are shaped. (If the cookies become too brittle, return them to the oven for a couple of minutes until they are hot and flexible again.)

If baking on nonstick foil, here's a trick for shaping a whole sheet of tuiles at the same time: Carefully grasp the edges of the foil as soon as the sheet comes from the oven (without touching the hot pan or the cookies) and roll the foil into a fat cylinder, gently curving the attached cookies like potato chips. Crimp or secure the foil with a paper clip. When the tuiles are cool, unroll the foil carefully and remove them.

ALMOND TUILES

Crispy, crunchy almond cookies are elegantly thin and buttery. They partner perfectly with creamy desserts like custards, pudding, and ice cream. Classic tuiles are cooled over a rolling pin (see the box on page 45 for methods, including a shortcut) to make them resemble the roof tiles they are named for, but you can also skip that step and make them flat.

Note: Small measures of flour vary too much in weight for delicate cookies. A scale is best. If you do not have a scale, firmly packed and leveled measures will get as close as possible to the correct weights for this particular recipe.

MAKES ABOUT FORTY 3-INCH COOKIES

---

2 tablespoons (28 grams) unsalted butter, melted, plus more for greasing the mats

2 large egg whites

2 teaspoons water

½ cup (100 grams) sugar

4 firmly packed tablespoons (44 grams) white rice flour
—OR—
5 firmly packed tablespoons (44 grams) Thai white rice flour

¼ teaspoon pure almond extract

Scant ½ teaspoon salt

⅔ cup (70 grams) sliced almonds

EQUIPMENT

Baking sheets

continued

Line the baking sheets with silicone mats or nonstick foil (nonstick side up). For mats, grease them with a very thin (but thorough) coat of melted butter. For nonstick foil, simply smooth the foil to eliminate creases.

In a medium bowl, mix the egg whites with the water, sugar, rice flour, almond extract, and salt until well blended. Stir in the butter and almonds. Cover the bowl and let the batter rest for several hours or overnight in the refrigerator to let the flour absorb moisture.

Position racks in the upper and lower thirds of the oven (or one rack in the center if you are baking only one sheet at a time) and preheat the oven to 325°F.

Stir the batter. Drop level teaspoons 2 inches apart on the prepared baking sheets. Use the back of the spoon to smear the batter into 2½-inch rounds. Bake, watching carefully, for 12 to 15 minutes, rotating the pans from top to bottom and from front to back about halfway through the baking time, until the tuiles are

Silicone baking mats or nonstick foil

Rolling pin or small cups for shaping (optional; see the box on page 45)

mostly deep golden brown. If the cookies are not baked enough, they will not be completely crisp when cool.

For flat cookies, you can simply slide the mats or foil sheets onto racks and let the cookies cool on them. Or, if you need to reuse the mats, wait a minute or two, then transfer the hot cookies to a rack to cool.

To retain crispness, put the cookies in an airtight container as soon as they are cool. They will keep for at least 1 month.

VARIATIONS

Oat and Almond Tuiles

Substitute ¼ cup plus 1 tablespoon, both firmly packed (44 grams), gluten-free oat flour for the white rice flour.

Oat and Coconut Tuiles

Substitute ¼ cup plus 1 tablespoon, both firmly packed (44 grams), gluten-free oat flour for the white rice flour and substitute ⅓ cup (25 grams) unsweetened dried shredded coconut for the almonds.

CHUNKY DOUBLE-CHOCOLATE COCONUT MERINGUES

Add coconut flakes, salted almonds, and chunks of bittersweet and creamy coconut-flavored white chocolate to a light meringue cookie, and you get a riot of creamy, crunchy, chewy, sweet, and salty in every bite. **MAKES 45 TO 50 COOKIES**

1 cup (140 grams) roasted salted almonds, coarsely chopped

4 ounces (115 grams) 70% cacao dark chocolate, cut into chunks, or ⅔ cup purchased chocolate chunks or chips

1 cup (40 grams) unsweetened dried flaked coconut (coconut chips)

2 ounces (60 grams) coconut white chocolate (such as Lindt), cut into ⅓-inch squares

3 large egg whites, at room temperature

⅛ teaspoon cream of tartar

½ cup plus 2 tablespoons (125 grams) sugar

EQUIPMENT

Stand mixer with whisk attachment, or handheld mixer

2 baking sheets, lined with parchment paper

Position racks in the upper and lower thirds of the oven and preheat the oven to 200°F.

In a small bowl, combine one-quarter of the almonds, dark chocolate, and coconut for sprinkling. Set aside.

In a medium bowl, mix the remaining almonds, chocolate, and coconut with the coconut white chocolate. Set aside.

Combine the egg whites and cream of tartar in the bowl of the stand mixer fitted with the whisk attachment (or in a large bowl if using a handheld mixer). Beat on medium-high speed (or on high speed with the handheld mixer) until the egg whites are creamy white and hold a soft shape when the beaters are lifted. Continue to beat on medium to high speed, adding the sugar a little at a time, for 1½ to 2 minutes, until the egg whites are very stiff and have a dull sheen. Use a large rubber spatula to fold in the mixture of nuts, coconut, and both chocolates, just until blended. Do not let the batter sit.

Drop generous tablespoons of meringue 1½ inches apart on the prepared baking sheets. Make sure all the batter fits on the two sheets so all the meringues can be baked at once; if necessary, make each cookie a little bigger. Sprinkle the meringues with the reserved chocolate, almonds, and coconut.

continued

Bake for 1½ hours, rotating the pans from top to bottom and from front to back halfway through the baking time. Remove a "test" meringue and let it cool completely before taking a bite. (Meringues are never crisp when hot.) If the test meringue is completely dry and crisp, turn off the oven and let the remaining meringues cool completely in the oven. If the test meringue is soft or chewy or sticks to your teeth, bake for another 15 to 30 minutes before cooling in the oven.

To prevent the cookies from becoming sticky, put them in an airtight container as soon as they are cool. They will keep for at least 2 weeks.

CHESTNUT AND WALNUT MERINGUES

Meringues come together quickly but require lots of time in the oven, so plan accordingly. Meringues also keep well, so you can have cookies, mushrooms (see the variation), or the makings of a fabulous dessert (just add ice cream, whipped cream, berries, and/or chocolate sauce) on hand at all times. **MAKES ABOUT 2½ DOZEN COOKIES**

¼ cup (25 grams) chestnut flour

¾ cup (75 grams) walnut pieces, coarsely chopped

¾ cup (150 grams) sugar

3 large egg whites, at room temperature

¼ teaspoon cream of tartar

EQUIPMENT

Stand mixer with whisk attachment

2 baking sheets, lined with parchment paper

Position racks in the upper and lower thirds of the oven and preheat the oven to 200°F.

In a small bowl, mix the chestnut flour and walnuts with ⅓ cup (65 grams) of the sugar.

Combine the egg whites and cream of tartar in the bowl of the stand mixer fitted with the whisk attachment and beat on medium-high speed until the egg whites are creamy white and hold a soft shape when the beaters are lifted. Continue to beat on high speed, adding the remaining sugar a little at a time over 1½ to 2 minutes, until the egg whites are very stiff.

Pour the chestnut flour mixture over the egg whites and fold in with a rubber spatula just until combined. Do not let the batter sit.

Drop heaping tablespoons of meringue 1½ inches apart onto the prepared baking sheets. Make sure all the batter fits on the two sheets so all the meringues can be baked at once; if necessary, make each cookie a little bigger.

Bake for 1½ hours. Rotate the pans from top to bottom and from front to back halfway through the baking time. Remove a "test" cookie and let it cool completely before taking a bite. (Meringues are never crisp when hot.) If the meringue is completely dry and crisp, turn off the heat and let the remaining meringues cool completely in the oven. If the test meringue is soft or chewy or sticks to your teeth, bake for another 15 to 30 minutes before testing again.

To prevent the meringues from becoming moist and sticky, put them in an airtight container as soon as they are cool. They will keep for at least 2 weeks.

VARIATION: Chestnut Meringue Mushrooms

Make the meringue as directed, omitting the walnuts. Scrape the meringue into a pastry bag fitted with a plain tip with a ½-inch opening. Pipe pointed "kisses" about 1 inch high to make "stems." Do not worry if the tips bend over or sag. Pipe domes to make mushroom "caps." Sieve a light dusting of unsweetened cocoa powder over the caps and stems and fan them or blow on them vigorously to blur the cocoa and give the mushrooms an authentic look. Bake as directed. If not assembling immediately, store the caps and stems in an airtight container as soon as they are cool.

To assemble the mushrooms, place 2 ounces (55 grams) chopped milk or dark chocolate in a small stainless steel bowl set in a skillet of barely simmering water. Immediately turn off the heat and stir the chocolate until it is melted and smooth.

Use a sharp knife to cut ¼ to ½ inch off the tip of each stem to create a flat surface. Spread a generous coat of melted chocolate over the flat side of several mushroom caps. Allow the chocolate to set partially before attaching the cut surface of the stems. Repeat until all the mushrooms are assembled. Set the mushrooms aside until the chocolate has hardened and the caps and stems are "glued" together. Store in an airtight container, as soon as possible. Makes about 40 mushrooms with 1¼-inch caps.

TOASTY PECAN BISCOTTI

These gorgeous spicy, nut-studded cookies are technically biscotti since they are baked twice (once on each side), and they have all the crunch of regular biscotti, but their nutty coating makes them extra crunchy and even more irresistible. They are delicious served on their own, but you can also use them to turn a simple dish of poached fruit, such as apples or pears, into a stunning dessert. **MAKES 16 BISCOTTI**

⅔ cup (100 grams) white rice flour
—OR—
1 cup (100 grams) Thai white rice flour

¼ cup plus 2 tablespoons (50 grams) sorghum flour

¼ cup (50 grams) granulated sugar

⅛ teaspoon xanthan gum

1 teaspoon baking powder

¼ teaspoon salt

¼ cup plus 2 tablespoons milk (any percent fat)

8 tablespoons (1 stick/ 115 grams) unsalted butter, softened

¼ cup (50 grams) coarse sugar, such as turbinado

½ teaspoon cinnamon (preferably canela cinnamon)

2 cups (200 grams) coarsely chopped pecans

continued

Combine the rice and sorghum flours, granulated sugar, xanthan gum, baking powder, salt, and milk in the bowl of the stand mixer fitted with the paddle attachment and beat for 2 minutes; the dough will be very stiff. It is important to beat the dough long enough or the biscotti won't hold together; don't worry about overbeating. Add the butter and beat until thoroughly incorporated. Scrape the dough into a flat patty, wrap in plastic, and refrigerate for about 2 hours, until firm.

Position a rack in the upper third of the oven and preheat the oven to 400°F.

Combine the coarse sugar, cinnamon, and pecans in a bowl and scoop about half of the mixture onto the parchment paper on the baking sheet. Turn the dough patty out onto the mixture and turn and press it to cover both sides with nuts. Place it in the center of the paper and cover with another piece of parchment. Roll out to an 8-by-10-inch rectangle about ½ inch thick. Peel off the top sheet of parchment and pat or roll the remaining nut mixture onto the dough. Using a long thin knife, cut the dough straight down to make 2 sections, each 5 by 8 inches, then cut each section into 8 bars, 1 inch wide and 5 inches long. Wipe the knife with a paper towel as needed. Use the knife or

EQUIPMENT

Stand mixer with paddle attachment

Baking sheet, lined with parchment paper

Rolling pin

a spatula to move the bars so that they are evenly spaced on the same sheet. Press any stray nuts into the bars. Bake for 15 minutes. Remove from the oven and turn the biscotti over with a spatula, moving the browner ones to the center of the pan. Return to the oven and bake for 8 to 10 minutes, until the biscotti are lightly browned on top and bottom. Set the pan on a rack to cool. The biscotti will keep in an airtight container for several days.

CUTOUT COOKIES

When you need simple tasty cutout cookies for a child's party or a themed occasion, these are a sure thing. To decorate, simply sprinkle them with colored sugar before baking, or bake and cool the cookies first and then ice them—or pipe melted chocolate on them—before affixing sugars, sprinkles, miniature candies, and so on (see the box on pages 62–63). For simpler slice-and-bake cookies, see the sablé variations. **MAKES ABOUT 3 DOZEN 2½-INCH COOKIES**

1¼ cups plus 2 tablespoons (140 grams) gluten-free oat flour

¼ cup plus 2 tablespoons (55 grams) white rice flour
—OR—
½ cup plus 1 tablespoon (55 grams) Thai white rice flour

¼ teaspoon salt

⅛ teaspoon baking soda

⅔ cup (130 grams) sugar

¼ cup (60 grams) cream cheese, cut into chunks

12 tablespoons (1½ sticks/ 170 grams) unsalted butter, softened and cut into chunks

1 teaspoon pure vanilla extract

Gluten-free oat flour for cutting out the cookies

Colored sugars for sprinkling (optional—see the box on pages 62–63 for decorating inspiration)

continued

To make the dough by hand, put the oat and rice flours, salt, and baking soda in a large bowl and whisk until thoroughly blended. Add the sugar, cream cheese, butter, and vanilla. Use a fork or the back of a large spoon to mash and mix the ingredients together until all are blended into a smooth, soft dough.

To make the dough in a food processor, put the oat and rice flours, salt, and baking soda in the food processor. Pulse to mix. Add the sugar, cream cheese, butter, and vanilla. Pulse until the mixture forms a smooth, soft dough. Scrape the bowl and blend in any stray flour at the bottom with your fingers.

Form the dough into 2 flat patties. Wrap and refrigerate the dough for at least 2 hours, but preferably overnight (see Note).

Position racks in the upper and lower thirds of the oven and preheat the oven to 325°F.

Remove 1 patty from the refrigerator and let it sit at room temperature briefly, until supple enough to roll but still quite firm. It will continue to soften as you work. Roll the dough between two pieces of wax or parchment paper, or between heavy plastic sheets cut from a plastic bag, to a thickness of ⅛ inch. Turn the

NOTE: *Instead of chilling the dough first and rolling it later, you can roll the freshly made dough gently (it will be very soft) between sheets of wax or parchment paper immediately, then stack and refrigerate the rolled-out dough on a baking sheet for at least 2 hours or until needed.*

dough over once or twice while rolling it out to check for deep wrinkles; if necessary, peel off and smooth the paper or plastic over the dough before continuing to roll it. When the dough is thin enough, peel off the top sheet of paper or plastic and keep it in front of you. (If the dough is sticky, dust it with a little oat flour.) Invert the dough onto the sheet in front of you and peel off the second sheet.

Cut cookie shapes as close together as possible to minimize scraps, dipping the edges of the cookie cutters in oat flour as necessary to prevent sticking. Use the point of a paring knife to lift and remove scraps as you transfer cookies to the prepared baking sheets. Place the cookies ½ inch apart. If the dough gets too soft at any time—while rolling, cutting, removing scraps between cookies, or transferring cookies—slide a baking sheet underneath the paper or plastic and refrigerate the dough for a few minutes until firm. Repeat with the second piece of dough.

Press all the dough scraps together gently and reroll them as necessary. (Don't worry that rerolling scraps will produce tough cookies.) Sprinkle the cookies with colored sugars, if desired, and pat to adhere.

Bake for 8 to 12 minutes, until golden brown at the edges but deep brown on the bottom, rotating the pans from top to bottom and from front to back halfway through the baking time. Repeat until all the cookies are baked.

Set the pans or just the liners on racks to cool. Cool the cookies completely before icing, stacking, or storing. They will keep in an airtight container for at least 2 weeks.

continued

Slice-and-Bake Oat Sablés

Follow the instructions for making the dough, then scrape the dough onto a sheet of wax or parchment paper and form it into a 10-inch log about 1¾ inches in diameter. Wrap it tightly in the wax or parchment paper and refrigerate for at least 2 hours, but preferably longer or overnight. (The dough may be frozen for up to 3 months.) Use a sharp knife to cut the cold dough log into ¼-inch-thick slices. Place the cookies at least 1½ inches apart on the prepared baking sheets. Bake for 15 to 20 minutes, until the cookies are golden brown at the edges and well browned on the bottom. Rotate the pans from top to bottom and from front to back halfway through the baking time. Set the pans or just the liners on racks to cool. Cool the cookies completely before stacking or storing. They will keep in an airtight container for at least 2 weeks.

Nutty Oat Sablés

Add ½ cup (70 grams) of any raw or toasted nuts to the dough: If mixing by hand, add them to the dough at the end. If using a food processor, add nuts whole with the dry ingredients and pulse until they are the desired consistency. Proceed as directed in the main recipe if making cutout cookies, or the Slice-and-Bake Oat Sablés variation if you prefer to simply slice and bake the cookies.

Nibby Oat Sablés

Add a generous ¼ cup (35 grams) roasted cacao nibs to the dough with the butter. Proceed as directed in the main recipe if making cutout cookies, or the Slice-and-Bake Oat Sablés variation if you prefer to simply slice and bake the cookies.

Orange Sablés with Ancho Chile

Omit the vanilla and add 1½ teaspoons finely grated orange zest and 1½ teaspoons crumbled or powdered dried ancho chile with the butter. Proceed as directed in the main recipe if making cutout cookies, or the Slice-and-Bake Oat Sablés variation if you prefer to simply slice and bake the cookies.

Chai Sablés

Add 2 teaspoons pulverized chai (from a package of loose chai or from the contents of 2 to 3 chai tea bags) with the butter. Proceed as directed in the main recipe if making cutout cookies, or the Slice-and-Bake Oat Sablés variation if you prefer to simply slice and bake the cookies.

DECORATING COOKIES

Decorating with Sugar and Sprinkles

You can sprinkle unbaked cookies with colorful sugar just before baking. Or add colorful sugar or sprinkles to cookies decorated with icing or melted chocolate as described below.

Decorating with Chocolate

For piped or drizzled cookie decorations that dry hard and taste great, nothing beats pure melted chocolate. It's simple to use (although it must be kept warm, and no moisture can be allowed to touch it) and requires no tempering as long as you drizzle or pipe onto rather than dip or coat the surface of cookies. (Drizzled and piped chocolate will usually dry without discoloring, but chocolate that is spread all over the surface or used for dipping will turn gray and streaky if not tempered.) Use chocolate bars or wafers or disks that are meant to be melted; chocolate chips do not melt well enough for this purpose. You may tint white chocolate with oil-based or powdered food colors designed especially for chocolate—regular water-based food colors are not compatible with chocolate.

To melt the chocolate for decorating, chop 3 ounces of chocolate (dark, milk, or white) into small pieces and place in a small, dry heatproof (preferably stainless steel) bowl. Bring a wide skillet with about ½ inch of water to a simmer, then turn it off. Set the bowl of chocolate in the water and stir with a dry spatula until the chocolate is melted and smooth. Or melt the chocolate in a microwave-safe container on medium or 50% power for dark chocolate (low or 30% power for milk or white chocolate) for 2 minutes. Stir well. Microwave a few more seconds at a time, as necessary, stirring well, until the chocolate is melted and smooth.

Drizzle the chocolate over cookies with a spoon or fork, or pipe it from the corner of a small plastic decorating bag or zipper-type plastic bag (fill it, close it, snip off the tip, and squeeze from the top). Top the chocolate drizzles with sprinkles, if desired, while the chocolate is still soft. Let chocolate set and harden before storing cookies between layers of wax paper. If the chocolate begins to harden in the bag, microwave on low power for 10 seconds at a time until the chocolate is warm and flowing again.

Decorating with Icing

Simple powdered-sugar icing is easy to make and versatile. You can color it with ordinary food colors and/or flavor it with extracts or oils. Spread it on with a small spatula, paint it on with a brush, or pipe it from the corner of a small plastic decorating bag or zipper-type plastic bag (fill it, close it, snip off the tip, and squeeze from the top). Top icing with sprinkles, if desired. Let icing set and harden before storing between layers of wax paper.

To make ¾ cup of powdered sugar icing for cookies, mix 3 cups (12 ounces) powdered sugar with 2 to 3 tablespoons of water, lemon juice (for lemon-flavored icing,), or 4 to 5 tablespoons of brandy or rum to the desired consistency. Adjust by adding powdered sugar or liquid. If you like, flavor to taste with drops of extracts or flavor oils and/or tint with ordinary food coloring. Note that food coloring intensifies with time, so tint icing lighter than you think it should be.

QUINCE AND ORANGE–FILLED CHESTNUT COOKIES

With a filling of quince paste (available in better supermarkets or specialty stores) mixed with chopped candied orange peel or some grated orange zest, these homemade cookies look fancy on a holiday dessert bar. You can make a date variation by substituting chopped moist dates (such as medjools) for the quince paste. **MAKES 20 TO 24 COOKIES**

FOR THE DOUGH

1½ cups (150 grams) chestnut flour

⅓ cup plus 1 tablespoon (60 grams) white rice flour
—OR—
½ cup plus 1 tablespoon (60 grams) Thai white rice flour

½ cup (100 grams) sugar

Scant ½ teaspoon salt

12 tablespoons (1½ sticks/ 170 grams) unsalted butter, slightly softened, cut into chunks

¼ cup (60 grams) cream cheese

FOR THE FILLING

⅔ cup (180 grams) quince paste

¼ cup (40 grams) finely chopped candied orange peel, or additional quince paste

Grated zest of ½ orange, if not using candied orange peel (optional)

Powdered sugar for dusting

To make the dough by hand, put the chestnut and rice flours, sugar, and salt in a large bowl and whisk until thoroughly blended. Add the butter chunks and cream cheese. Use a fork or the back of a large spoon to mash and mix the ingredients together until all are blended into a smooth, soft dough.

To make the dough in a food processor, put the chestnut and rice flours, sugar, and salt in the food processor. Pulse to mix. Add the butter chunks and cream cheese. Pulse until the mixture forms a smooth, soft dough. Scrape the bowl and blend in any stray flour at the bottom of the bowl with your fingers.

Press the dough into a ball, wrap it in plastic, and refrigerate it for at least 2 hours, but preferably overnight and up to 3 days. (Or, to save work later, you can fill and shape the cookies immediately and *then* refrigerate them in a covered container for at least 2 hours.)

To make the filling, mash the quince paste with a fork and mix it with the candied orange peel or additional quince paste and orange zest. Shape level teaspoons (8 grams) of the quince paste into little balls (about ¾ inch in diameter) and set them on a plate or piece of wax or parchment paper.

continued

continued

Position racks in the upper and lower thirds of the oven and preheat the oven to 325°F.

Remove the dough from the refrigerator and let it soften for 10 or 15 minutes. Shape level tablespoons of dough (20 to 25 grams) into balls about 1¼ inches in diameter. Make a deep depression in the dough with a knuckle and widen it to form a little bowl. Press a ball of filling into the bowl and ease the dough up around the filling to completely enclose it. Set the cookie, seam side down, on the prepared baking sheets. You can leave the cookies round, or press them into a little beehive shape. Bake for 15 to 20 minutes, until the cookies are slightly golden brown and the bottoms are deep golden. Rotate the pans from top to bottom and from front to back a little over halfway through the baking time. Place the pans on racks, or slide the liners from the pans onto racks to cool. Sift a little powdered sugar over the cookies. Cool the cookies completely before stacking or storing. They will keep in an airtight container for at least 2 weeks. Resift with powdered sugar before serving, if desired.

WALNUT ALFAJORES

Alfajores are luscious sandwich cookies filled with dulce de leche or cajeta. Every region makes alfajores with a different type of cookie, so you should never hesitate to invent your own new combinations. Here, the sweet caramelized milk balances the bitter tannins in the walnuts perfectly. If you're a fan of Nutella, you can use it to fill the cookies instead of the dulce de leche.

MAKES TWENTY 2-INCH SANDWICH COOKIES

Scant ½ cup (50 grams) coconut flour

1½ cups (150 grams) walnut pieces

¼ teaspoon baking powder

½ teaspoon salt

1 cup plus 2 tablespoons (225 grams) sugar

6 tablespoons (85 grams) unsalted butter, very soft

1 teaspoon pure vanilla extract

1 large egg white

⅔ cup dulce de leche or cajeta (see Note, page 21)

EQUIPMENT

Food processor fitted with the steel blade

Baking sheets, lined with parchment paper

Put the coconut flour, walnuts, baking powder, salt, and sugar in the food processor. Process until the walnuts are finely ground, about 15 seconds. Add the butter, vanilla, and egg white and pulse 8 to 10 times, or until the dough comes together. Form the mixture into a 10-inch log 2 inches in diameter on a sheet of wax or parchment paper. Wrap the log in the paper, keeping it as cylindrical as possible. Chill for at least 2 hours and up to 3 days, or wrap airtight and freeze for up to 3 months. Thaw before using.

Position racks in the upper and lower thirds of the oven and preheat the oven to 350°F.

Use a thin serrated knife to cut the dough into slices a little less than ¼ inch thick. Place the slices 1 inch apart on the prepared baking sheets. Bake for 9 to 11 minutes, until the cookies are golden on the bottom and browned at the edges; rotate the pans from top to bottom and from front to back halfway through the baking time. Place the pans on racks, or slide the liners from the pans onto racks to cool completely.

continued

When the cookies are completely cool, fill with dulce de leche. Turn half of the cookies upside down. Spoon dulce de leche into one corner of a resealable plastic freezer bag. Clip about ¼ inch from the corner and pipe about 1½ teaspoons onto each upside-down cookie. Cover with a right-side-up cookie and press very gently to spread the filling toward the edges.

The filled cookies will keep in an airtight container for up to 3 days, although they will soften after the first day. Unfilled cookies may be stored for up to 1 week.

NUTELLA SANDWICH COOKIES

Shortbread cookies filled with chocolate-hazelnut spread—what's not to love? You can add ground hazelnuts to the cookie dough or not, as you like.

MAKES ABOUT 25 SANDWICH COOKIES

---

1 cup plus 2 tablespoons (150 grams) sorghum flour

⅓ cup plus 1 tablespoon (60 grams) white rice flour
—OR—
½ cup plus 1 tablespoon (60 grams) Thai white rice flour

⅔ cup (130 grams) granulated sugar

½ teaspoon salt

1 cup (140 grams) hazelnuts (optional)

12 tablespoons (1½ sticks/ 170 grams) unsalted butter, slightly softened, cut into chunks

¼ cup (60 grams) cream cheese

1 tablespoon water

1 teaspoon pure vanilla extract

Coarse sugar, such as turbinado, for rolling

¾ cup chocolate-hazelnut spread, such as Nutella

EQUIPMENT

Food processor fitted with the steel blade

Baking sheets, lined with parchment paper

Put the sorghum and rice flours, granulated sugar, salt, and hazelnuts, if using, in the food processor and pulse until the hazelnuts are finely ground. Add the butter chunks, cream cheese, water, and vanilla. Pulse until the mixture forms a smooth, soft dough. Scrape the bowl and blend in any stray flour at the bottom of the bowl with your fingers. On a sheet of wax or parchment paper, shape the dough into a 12-inch log about 2 inches in diameter. Wrap the dough and refrigerate it for at least 2 hours, but preferably overnight.

Position racks in the upper and lower thirds of the oven and preheat the oven to 325°F.

Roll the chilled cookie dough in the coarse sugar, pressing it to adhere. Cut into slices less than ¼ inch thick and place them 1 inch apart on the prepared baking sheets. Bake for 20 to 25 minutes, until the cookies are golden brown at the edges. Rotate the pans from top to bottom and from front to back a little over halfway through the baking time. Place the pans on racks, or slide the liners from the pans onto racks to cool. Cool the cookies completely before stacking, filling, or storing. Unfilled cookies will keep in an airtight container for at least 2 weeks.

Turn half of the cookies upside down. Spoon the chocolate-hazelnut spread into one corner of a resealable plastic freezer bag. Clip about ¼ inch

from the corner and pipe about 1½ teaspoons onto each upside-down cookie. Cover with a right-side-up cookie and press very gently to spread the filling toward the edges. The filled cookies will keep in an airtight container for up to 3 days, although they will soften after the first few hours.

CHOCOLATE SABLÉS

These super-simple slice-and-bake shortbread cookies are only slightly sweet, but they have great cocoa flavor and a beautiful dark color. While they are completely addictive with nothing added, you can dress them up endlessly. If you want fancier-looking cookies for holiday parties or gifts (or something fun to do with children), you can roll the dough into balls, dredge with sugar, and flatten them individually before baking (see Note), or you can roll out the dough for cutout cookies to decorate. Try the extra-bittersweet variation for even more chocolate flavor, and don't miss the Chocolate-Mint Sandwich Cookies variation. **MAKES ABOUT 40 COOKIES**

1 cup plus 2 tablespoons (150 grams) teff flour

⅓ cup plus 1 tablespoon (60 grams) white rice flour
—OR—
½ cup plus 1 tablespoon (60 grams) Thai white rice flour

¼ cup plus 2 tablespoons (35 grams) natural unsweetened cocoa powder

⅔ cup (135 grams) sugar

Scant ½ teaspoon salt

⅛ teaspoon baking soda

12 tablespoons (1½ sticks/ 170 grams) unsalted butter, slightly softened and cut into chunks

¼ cup (60 grams) cream cheese

1 tablespoon water

1 teaspoon pure vanilla extract

To make the dough by hand, put the teff and rice flours, cocoa, sugar, salt, and baking soda in a large bowl and whisk until thoroughly blended. Add the butter chunks, cream cheese, water, and vanilla. Use a fork or the back of a large spoon to mash and mix the ingredients together until all are blended into a smooth, soft dough.

To make the dough in a food processor, put the teff and rice flours, cocoa, sugar, salt, and baking soda in the food processor. Pulse to mix. Add the butter chunks, cream cheese, water, and vanilla. Pulse until the mixture forms a smooth, soft dough. Scrape the bowl and blend in any stray flour at the bottom of the bowl with your fingers.

On a sheet of wax or parchment paper, shape the dough into a 10-inch log about 2 inches in diameter. Wrap the dough and refrigerate it for at least 2 hours, but preferably overnight.

Position racks in the upper and lower thirds of the oven and preheat the oven to 325°F.

continued

continued

Slice the chilled cookie dough into ¼-inch slices and place them 1 inch apart on the lined sheets. Bake for 20 to 25 minutes, or until the cookies are firm to the touch (it is hard to tell by looking, but flip one cookie over and see if it is slightly browned on the bottom). Rotate the pans from top to bottom and from front to back a little over halfway through the baking time. Place the pans on racks, or slide the liners from the pans onto racks to cool. Cool the cookies completely before stacking or storing. The cookies will keep in an airtight container for at least 2 weeks.

NOTE: *If you have time to be a little fussier, you can shape chilled dough into 1-inch balls and roll them in sugar before placing them 2 inches apart on the lined baking sheets. Flatten each ball to about ¼ inch by covering with a piece of wax paper and pressing with a flat-bottomed cup; peel off the wax paper and repeat with the remaining cookies. Bake as directed.*

Spicy Chocolate Sablés

Add ¾ teaspoon ground cinnamon and ⅛ teaspoon each ground cayenne and freshly ground black pepper with the dry ingredients.

Extra-Bittersweet Chocolate Sablés

Put half of the sugar in the processor with 1½ ounces (45 grams) coarsely chopped unsweetened chocolate or a high-percentage cacao (70% or higher) dark chocolate. Pulse until the chocolate pieces are the size of sesame seeds. Add the remaining ingredients and proceed as directed. These cookies take extra time to crisp up after they are cool because the chocolate takes longer to set and harden.

Chocolate-Mint Sandwich Cookies

Melt 4 ounces (115 grams) dark, milk, or white chocolate (see page 62) and flavor with 2 drops (use an eye dropper!) of mint oil. Don't use mint extract or any non-oil-based flavoring or the chocolate will seize. Taste and adjust the flavor with additional drops of mint oil if necessary.

Sandwich cookies with ½ teaspoon of the minty chocolate. Let them stand to set the chocolate before serving.

BUCKWHEAT LINZER COOKIES

These pretty cookies look as though they are fussy to make, but they are actually slice-and-bake cookies, with holes cut from half of them about halfway through the baking time. Buckwheat pairs well with any dark berry or cherry flavor, so feel free to try different preserves. The cookies keep well, but they should be assembled only shortly before serving. Leftover filled cookies will soften a bit, but they will still taste great. **MAKES ABOUT 1½ DOZEN 2-INCH SANDWICH COOKIES**

Buckwheat Shortbread Cookies dough (page 34), shaped into a log and chilled as directed

¼ cup blackberry (or other) preserves

Powdered sugar for dusting

EQUIPMENT

Food processor fitted with the steel blade (optional)

Baking sheets, lined with parchment paper

⅞-inch round cookie cutter (or bottle cap to improvise)

Fine-mesh strainer

Position racks in the upper and lower thirds of the oven and preheat the oven to 325°F.

Slice the chilled log less than ¼ inch thick and place the slices 1½ inches apart on the prepared baking sheets, dividing the total number equally between them. Bake for about 12 minutes. Remove the upper sheet of cookies and place it on the counter or stovetop. Press the cookie cutter gently into each cookie. If the centers lift out, fine; otherwise you can remove them later. Switch and rotate the pans, placing the first on the lower rack in place of the second. Bake for 10 to 15 minutes, or until the cookies are slightly darker at the edges and well browned on the bottom.

Set the pans or just the liners on racks to cool. Cool the cookies completely. Remove the cutouts. Unfilled cookies will keep in an airtight container for at least 2 weeks.

Shortly before serving, spread ½ teaspoon preserves on each of the cookies without holes. Sieve a little powdered sugar over the cookies with holes and place one on top of each jam-topped cookie.

APRICOT WALNUT RUGELACH

Part of a great eastern European Jewish baking tradition, rugelach, though considered cookies, are really miniature pastries: flaky cream cheese dough rolled up around cinnamon sugar, jam, currants, and nuts (the traditional filling), or fanciful variations that may include bits of chocolate or cacao nibs or whatever good things a baker might have on hand. Not surprisingly, the oat flour is a perfect flavor partner for the fruits, nuts, and spices in this recipe and all the variations. **MAKES 4 DOZEN COOKIES**

FOR THE DOUGH

½ pound (2 sticks/225 grams) unsalted butter, cold

1⅓ cups (200 grams) white rice flour, plus more for rolling
—OR—
2 cups (200 grams) Thai white rice flour, plus more for rolling

1¾ cups (175 grams) gluten-free oat flour

8 ounces (225 grams) cream cheese

2 tablespoons (25 grams) sugar

1 teaspoon xanthan gum

½ teaspoon baking soda

¼ teaspoon salt

¼ cup water, plus more as needed

FOR THE FILLING

¾ cup (235 grams) thick apricot jam or preserves

1 teaspoon ground cinnamon

continued

To make the dough, using the largest holes on a box (or other) grater, grate the butter onto a plate lined with wax paper. Refrigerate until needed.

Combine the rice and oat flours in a small bowl and mix thoroughly with a whisk.

In the bowl of the stand mixer fitted with the paddle attachment or in a large bowl with a handheld mixer, mix the cream cheese, sugar, xanthan gum, baking soda, salt, and water for about 2 minutes on medium speed. The mixture will look wet and stretchy.

Add the flour mixture and beat on low speed until the mixture resembles coarse bread crumbs (it will not be smooth). Sprinkle the shredded butter into the bowl and mix on low speed to break the butter shreds into bits and distribute them. The mixture will resemble loose crumbs, sticking together only when pinched. If necessary, sprinkle and mix in another tablespoon of water. Do not try to form a cohesive dough. Divide the mixture into quarters. Dump one-quarter in the center of a sheet of plastic wrap. Bring the sides of the wrap up around the mixture on all sides, pressing firmly to form a patty about 5 inches in diameter. Wrap the

1 cup (225 grams) finely chopped walnuts

½ cup (65 grams) chopped dried apricots

Salt

Cinnamon sugar: 2 tablespoons sugar mixed with ½ teaspoon ground cinnamon

EQUIPMENT

Box grater

Stand mixer with paddle attachment or handheld mixer

Rolling pin

Baking sheets, lined with parchment paper or foil

Food processor (optional)

patty tightly. Repeat with the remaining 3 portions of dough. Refrigerate the patties until firm, at least 2 hours and up to 3 days.

Position racks in the upper and lower thirds of the oven and preheat the oven to 350°F.

Remove 1 piece of dough from the refrigerator. If necessary, let it stand until pliable enough to roll but not too soft. Roll between sheets of wax or parchment paper into a 12-inch round a scant ⅛ inch thick. Slide the wax paper and dough onto a baking sheet and refrigerate. Repeat with the remaining pieces of dough, stacking them in the refrigerator. Chill the dough for at least 15 minutes. Meanwhile, to make the filling, pulse the preserves in a food processor if there are large pieces of fruit and stir in the cinnamon.

Set one piece of dough on the counter and peel off the top sheet of wax paper and turn it clean side up on the counter or a cutting board. Dust the dough very lightly with a little rice flour and flip it onto the paper and peel off the second sheet. Spread one-quarter of the preserves over the dough and sprinkle with one-quarter of the walnuts, one-quarter of the apricots, and a tiny pinch of salt. Cut the dough like a pie into 12 equal wedges. Roll the wide outside edge up around the filling toward the point, brushing off any excess rice flour as you go. Place the roll, with the dough point underneath to prevent it from unrolling, on a prepared baking sheet. Repeat with the remaining wedges, placing cookies 1½ inches apart. If at times the dough becomes too soft to roll, return it to the refrigerator to firm up. Fill, cut, and roll the remaining pieces of dough. Sprinkle with cinnamon sugar.

Bake for 18 to 20 minutes, until the cookies are golden brown at the edges and deep brown on the bottom. Rotate the pans from top to bottom and from front to back halfway through the baking time. Set the pans or just the liners on racks to cool. Let the rugelach cool completely before stacking or storing. The rugelach are always most exquisite on the day they are baked, but they remain delicious, stored in an airtight container, for about 5 days.

VARIATIONS

Blueberry Walnut Rugelach

Omit the apricot preserves. Mix the walnuts and cinnamon with 2 tablespoons (25 grams) granulated sugar, ½ cup (100 grams) packed brown sugar, and ½ cup (70 grams) dried blueberries (or substitute currants). Sprinkle one-quarter of the mixture over each round of dough, and roll over the filling with a rolling pin to press it gently into the dough before cutting into wedges. Sprinkle with salt, roll up, and bake as directed.

Chocolate-Hazelnut Rugelach

Combine ½ cup (100 grams) granulated sugar, 1 teaspoon pure vanilla extract, 1 cup (225 grams) finely chopped toasted and skinned hazelnuts, and 1 cup (170 grams) miniature chocolate chips. Use in place of the apricot filling as follows: Sprinkle one-quarter of the mixture over each round of dough, and roll over the filling with a rolling pin to press it gently into the dough before cutting into wedges. Sprinkle with salt, roll up, and bake as directed.

continued

Cacao Nib Rugelach

Combine 2 tablespoons (25 grams) granulated sugar, ½ cup (100 grams) packed light brown sugar, 1 teaspoon ground cinnamon, ½ cup (70 grams) dried currants, and ½ cup (55 grams) roughly chopped cacao nibs for the walnuts. Use in place of the apricot filling as follows: Sprinkle one-quarter of the mixture over each round of dough, and roll over the filling with a rolling pin to press it gently into the dough before cutting into wedges. Sprinkle with salt, roll up, and bake as directed.

PEANUT CRUNCH BROWNIES

These very rich, very decadent brownies with a not-quite-grown-up flavor appeal to most grown-ups. **MAKES 25 SMALL BROWNIES**

FOR THE CHOCOLATE LAYER

8 tablespoons (1 stick/ 115 grams) unsalted butter, softened

4 ounces (115 grams) 66% to 72% cacao dark chocolate, coarsely chopped

1¼ cups (250 grams) granulated sugar

2 large eggs

1 teaspoon pure vanilla extract

¼ teaspoon salt

⅓ cup plus 1 tablespoon (60 grams) white rice flour —OR— ½ cup plus 1 tablespoon (60 grams) Thai white rice flour

FOR THE PEANUT CRUNCH LAYER

4 tablespoons (½ stick/ 55 grams) unsalted butter, softened

½ cup (100 grams) packed light brown sugar

¼ teaspoon salt

1 large egg

½ teaspoon pure vanilla extract

continued

Position a rack in the lower third of the oven and preheat the oven to 350°F.

To make the chocolate layer, place the butter and chocolate in a medium stainless steel bowl set directly in a wide skillet of barely simmering water. Stir frequently until the chocolate is completely melted and the mixture is smooth and quite hot to the touch. Stir in the sugar and remove from the heat. Use a large spoon to beat in the eggs, vanilla, and salt. The mixture should be very smooth; if it is not, place the bowl back in the water bath over very low heat for 30 seconds, stirring constantly. Add the flour and beat with a spoon until the batter comes away from the sides of the bowl, about 1 minute. Set aside.

To make the peanut crunch layer, in a separate bowl, use a large spoon or spatula to mix all the ingredients until completely blended. Press the mixture evenly in the bottom of the prepared pan. Bake for 8 to 10 minutes, until the batter is slightly darker at the edges.

Remove the pan from the oven and spoon dollops of chocolate batter all over the hot crust. Spread gently to make an even layer. Return the pan to the oven and bake for 20 to 22 minutes, until the surface is dry and pulls away slightly from the sides of the pan. Cool completely in the pan on a rack. Lift the edges of the pan liner and transfer the brownies to a cutting board.

continued

½ cup plus 2 tablespoons (160 grams) salted crunchy natural peanut butter

⅓ cup plus 1 tablespoon (60 grams) white rice flour —OR— ½ cup plus 1 tablespoon (60 grams) Thai white rice flour

¼ teaspoon baking soda

9-inch square metal baking pan, bottom and all four sides lined with foil

Cut into 25 squares. The brownies will keep in an airtight container for 3 to 4 days.

VARIATION: Hazelnut Crunch Brownies

Substitute 2 cups (160 grams) hazelnut meal/flour plus ½ teaspoon salt for the peanut butter.

GINGER-PEACH SQUARES

These festive cookies are both tenderly crunchy and a little chewy from the dried fruit and candied ginger filling. You can sprinkle some chopped pecans onto the dough with the filling to make fruit- and nut-filled squares instead.

MAKES TWENTY-FIVE 2-INCH COOKIES

---

1 cup plus 2 tablespoons (150 grams) sorghum flour

⅓ cup plus 1 tablespoon (60 grams) white rice flour, plus more for the dough
—OR—
½ cup plus 1 tablespoon (60 grams) Thai white rice flour, plus more for the dough

½ cup (100 grams) granulated sugar

Rounded ¼ teaspoon salt

12 tablespoons (1½ sticks/ 170 grams) unsalted butter, slightly softened and cut into chunks

¼ cup (60 grams) cream cheese

1 tablespoon water

1 teaspoon pure vanilla extract

1 cup (140 grams) diced dried peaches

3 tablespoons (30 grams) finely diced candied ginger

2 to 3 tablespoons coarse sugar, such as turbinado, for sprinkling

continued

To make the dough by hand, put the sorghum and rice flours, granulated sugar, and salt in a large bowl and whisk until thoroughly blended. Add the butter chunks, cream cheese, water, and vanilla. Use a fork or the back of a large spoon to mash and mix the ingredients together until all are blended into a smooth, soft dough.

To make the dough in a food processor, put the sorghum and rice flours, granulated sugar, and salt in the food processor and pulse to mix. Add the butter chunks, cream cheese, water, and vanilla. Pulse until the mixture forms a smooth, soft dough. Scrape the bowl and blend in any stray flour at the bottom of the bowl with your fingers.

Divide the dough in half. Use a dark pencil or a marker to draw a 10-by-10-inch square on each of two pieces of parchment paper. Turn one sheet upside down (to prevent the dough from touching the pencil or ink marks) on the counter and anchor the corners with tape.

Press and then spread (with a small offset spatula) one piece of the dough to make an even ¼-inch layer within the square. Check to be sure the center is not thicker than the edges. Remove the tape and slide the parchment onto a baking sheet. Distribute the peach

Whole nutmeg (optional, for grating)

EQUIPMENT

Food processor fitted with the steel blade (optional)

Baking sheets, both unlined and lined with parchment paper

pieces evenly over the dough, followed by the ginger pieces. Set aside.

Turn the second parchment sheet over and secure it to the counter. Spread the remaining dough over it as before and release the tape. Cover the fruit-topped dough with the second sheet of dough as follows: Place the pan with the fruit-topped dough next to the plain dough. Lift the far edge of the parchment under the plain dough until the dough dangles over the counter. Line up the dangling edge with the far edge of the fruit-topped dough. Let the edges touch, then lower the dough sheet toward you, to cover the fruit. (It's easier to do than to describe!) Don't peel the paper from the dough; just press very gently all over to adhere the dough and fruit. Put the baking sheet in the fridge and refrigerate for at least 2 hours, but preferably overnight.

Position racks in the upper and lower thirds of the oven and preheat the oven to 325°F.

Remove the dough from the refrigerator and peel the paper from the top. Dust the top of the dough and a cutting board very lightly with rice flour. Lift the parchment under the dough, flip the dough over onto the cutting board, and peel off the paper. Sprinkle with the coarse sugar, and grate a little nutmeg over the dough, if desired. Pat lightly to make sure the sugar adheres. Use a heavy knife to trim the edges. Use a straight-down "guillotine" stroke to cut 5 strips, then cut each strip into 5 pieces to make 25 pieces. Don't worry if the dough cracks when you cut it. Use a spatula to lift and place the cookies 1 inch apart on parchment paper–lined pans.

Bake for 15 to 20 minutes, until the cookies are golden brown at the edges and deep golden brown when you peek underneath (carefully, as the cookies are very fragile while hot). Rotate the pans from top to bottom and from front to back a little over halfway through the baking time. Place the pans on racks, or slide the liners from the pans onto racks to cool. Cool the cookies completely before stacking or storing. They will keep in an airtight container for at least a week.

RESOURCES

Allen Creek Farm

allencreekfarm.com

The best source for fresh, flavorful, extra-fine chestnut flour without any smoky flavor. They also make a coarser stone-ground chestnut flour. The recipes in this book use extra-fine flour.

Anson Mills

ansonmills.com

Rustic aromatic buckwheat flour.

Asian Grocery Stores

Asian grocery stores carry the most economical and finest grind of white rice flour, both regular and sweet white rice flour (also known as glutinous white rice flour) from Thailand. You can find Thai rice flour online at amazon.com or efooddepot.com. Look for the Erawan brand (marketed by Erawan Marketing in Bangkok), which we often use, or for the Flying Horse brand. Note that Thai rice flour bags are color-coded: red printing on the label for regular white rice flour that you can use for recipes in this book; green printing for sweet rice flour, which is not called for in this book.

Authentic Foods

authenticfoods.com

A great source for superfine flours: white and brown rice, white corn, sorghum, and more.

Bob's Red Mill

bobsredmill.com

Bob's Red Mill makes every kind of flour imaginable, including corn flour, oat flour, white and brown rice flour, coconut flour, sorghum flour, teff flour, and buckwheat flour, as well as xanthan gum. Their rice, sorghum, and corn flours are regular grind and may therefore give less light and delicate results than superfine flours in some recipes; however, they are completely acceptable unless otherwise indicated in the recipe.

King Arthur Flour

kingarthurflour.com

Baking utensils, scales, digital scales, parchment paper sheets, flours, xanthan gum, specialty sugars, and more.

Local Shops

Health food and natural food stores and high-end grocery stores carry special flours, nuts, and seeds in packages or in bulk. Big-box stores are also good sources. Restaurant supply stores are treasure troves for reasonably priced pans and utensils.

Market Hall Foods

markethallfoods.com

One of my favorite purveyors of specialty foods and ingredients, with retail stores in Oakland and Berkeley, California. Market Hall has a subspecialty in baking ingredients, including chocolates and cocoa, honeys, nuts, pastes, specialty sugars, preserves, a variety of chestnut products, and much more.

Oaktown Spice Shop

oaktownspiceshop.com

A welcome stop on a day of routine errands for those of us who are local, Oaktown's passionately sourced spices are freshly ground in the shop every week or two. It makes a world of difference! Whole and ground spices, specialty salts, and more are available in the Oakland and Berkeley shops and online.

Penzeys Spices

penzeys.com

This impeccable spice source sells every kind of herb, spice, and seasoning imaginable. The catalog alone is an education in flavor ingredients and their uses.

Sur La Table

surlatable.com

Purveyor of all kinds of baking supplies and utensils, including digital scales.

The Teff Company

teffco.com

Brown and ivory teff grains and flour, plus recipes, history, and information about teff.

INDEX

CONVERSION CHARTS

Here are rounded-off equivalents between the metric system and the traditional systems that are used in the United States to measure weight and volume.

FRACTIONS	DECIMALS
⅛	.125
¼	.25
⅓	.33
⅜	.375
½	.5
⅝	.625
⅔	.67
¾	.75
⅞	.875

WEIGHTS

US/UK	METRIC
¼ oz	7 g
½ oz	15 g
1 oz	30 g
2 oz	55 g
3 oz	85 g
4 oz	110 g
5 oz	140 g
6 oz	170 g
7 oz	200 g
8 oz (½ lb)	225 g
9 oz	250 g
10 oz	280 g
11 oz	310 g
12 oz	340 g
13 oz	370 g
14 oz	400 g
15 oz	425 g
16 oz (1 lb)	455 g

VOLUME

AMERICAN	IMPERIAL	METRIC
¼ tsp		1.25 ml
½ tsp		2.5 ml
1 tsp		5 ml
½ Tbsp (1½ tsp)		7.5 ml
1 Tbsp (3 tsp)		15 ml
¼ cup (4 Tbsp)	2 fl oz	60 ml
⅓ cup (5 Tbsp)	2½ fl oz	75 ml
½ cup (8 Tbsp)	4 fl oz	125 ml
⅔ cup (10 Tbsp)	5½ fl oz	150 ml
¾ cup (12 Tbsp)	6 fl oz	175 ml
1 cup (16 Tbsp)	8 fl oz	250 ml
1¼ cups	10 fl oz	300 ml
1½ cups	12 fl oz	350 ml
2 cups (1 pint)	16 fl oz	500 ml
2½ cups	20 fl oz (1 pint)	625 ml
5 cups	40 fl oz (1 qt)	1.25 l

OVEN TEMPERATURES

°F	°C	GAS MARK
250–275	130–140	½–1
300	148	2
325	163	3
350	177	4
375–400	190–204	5–6
425	218	7
450–475	232–245	8–9

Library of Congress Cataloging-in-Publication Data

Names: Medrich, Alice, author. | Klein, Maya, author. | Beisch, Leigh, photographer.
Title: The artisanal kitchen: gluten-free holiday cookies / Alice Medrich with Maya Klein ; photographs by Leigh Beisch.
Description: New York : Artisan, a division of Workman Publishing Co., Inc., 2020. | Includes index.
Identifiers: LCCN 2019048612 | ISBN 9781579659622 (hardcover)
Subjects: LCSH: Cookies. | Baking. | Gluten-free diet—Recipes. | Holiday cooking.
Classification: LCC TX772 .M4316 2020 | DDC 641.86/54—dc23
LC record available at https://lccn.loc.gov/2019048612

Cover design by Hanh Le
Interior design by Hanh Le, based on an original design by Laura Klynstra

Artisan books are available at special discounts when purchased in bulk for premiums and sales promotions as well as for fund-raising or educational use. Special editions or book excerpts also can be created to specification. For details, contact the Special Sales Director at the address below, or send an e-mail to specialmarkets@workman.com.

For speaking engagements, contact speakersbureau@workman.com.

Published by Artisan
A division of Workman Publishing Co., Inc.
225 Varick Street
New York, NY 10014-4381
artisanbooks.com

Artisan is a registered trademark of Workman Publishing Co., Inc.

This book has been adapted from *Gluten-Free Flavor Flours* (Artisan, 2014)

Published simultaneously in Canada by Thomas Allen & Son, Limited

Printed in China

First printing, August 2020

10 9 8 7 6 5 4 3 2 1